This book is dedicated to

Joseph Richard

Smith

who was born on

April 17, 2020

at

7:54pm

weighing
7
POUNDS
&
2
OUNCES

and was
21
INCHES
long

Mom's Baby Info

Birthday: 7/5/95

Time: 9:05am

Pounds: 6

Ounces: 4

Dad's Baby Info

Birthday: 8/16/94

Time: 8:16pm

Pounds: 8

Ounces: 1

Joseph, would it, could it, possibly be,
that I could love you more after we meet?

This thought truly puzzles me.

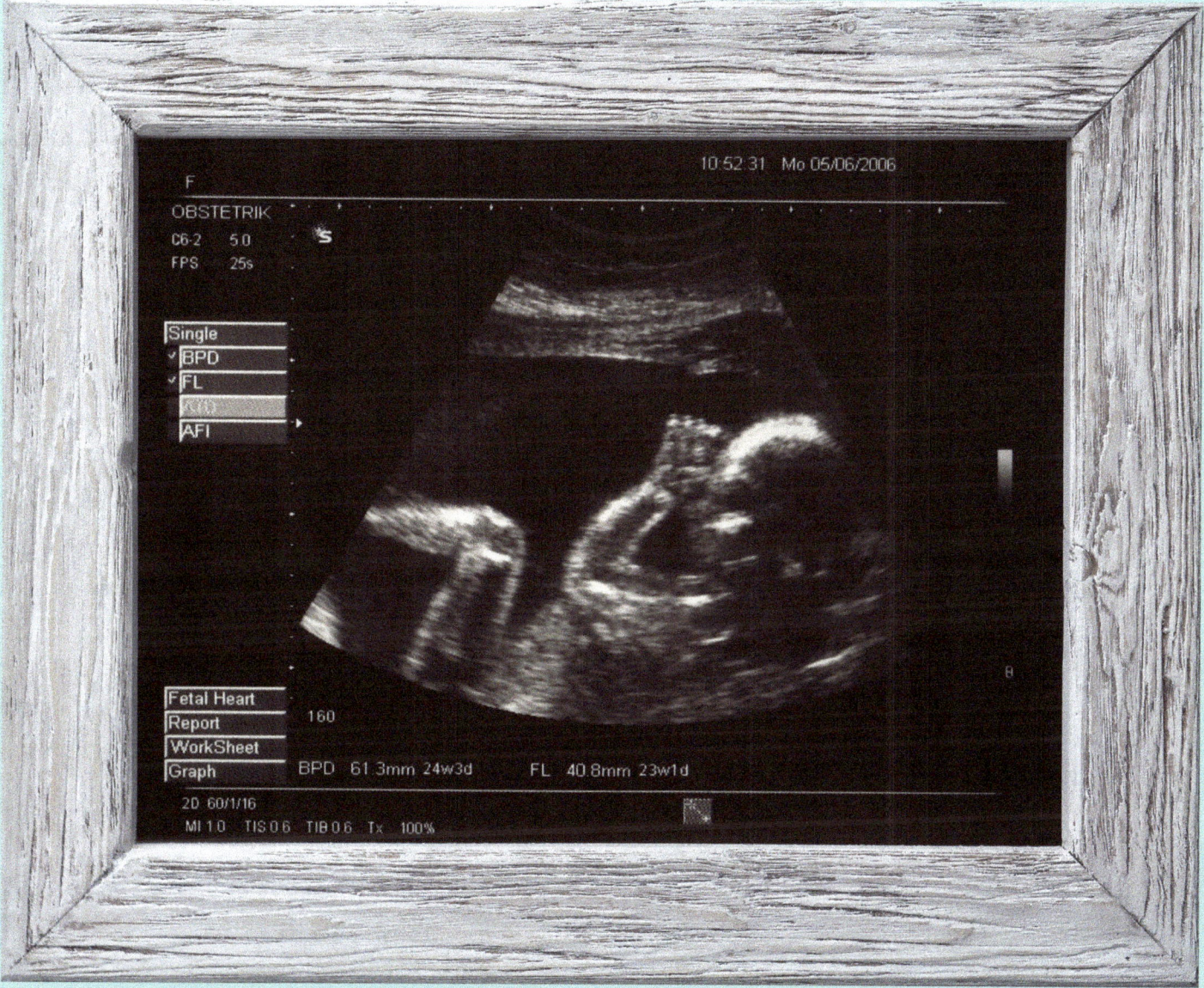

I have thought so much about the kind of young man you will one day be.

I want so much to see you, hear you, and feel your heart beat.

So I sit and stare at my swollen feet, wishing I were asleep so that my dreams could bring those things to me.

All day long I hear the birds sing, and it makes me wonder what your first sound might be.

Will it be a coo, a gurgle or a thunderous cry that you have chosen for me?

Whichever it is, a treasure it will be.

Baby's first sound

__Laugh__

Dad's first sound

__Wail__

Mom's first sound

__Cry__

At night, at last, my wish is granted to me. Fast asleep.

I can hear your heart beat and feel you breathe as I hold you close to me.

This sweet dream is so precious to me.

For when I look up, I can see your face the very first time you look at me.

But, Joseph, my son, the details aren't so clear to me. Are those your father's eyes or mine?

Is the hair on your head black, brown, blonde, or red? Is there any hair on your head at all?

These things are still a mystery to me.

Mommy

Daddy

Oh what a glorious dream this is for me. Those are my toes I can actually see!

I count your toes, there are 5 on both feet, and they are as cute as can be.

xoxo

xo

Kisses and hugs is what you get from everyone you meet.

But our most precious time, you will see, is when it is just you and me!

I will kiss you a million times, times three, and if you could talk you'd probably say to me, no more kisses mommy, please!

This dream for me has now become bitter and sweet, for I can actually smell how stinky your first diaper will be.

CAUTION

TOXIC
VAPORS

As I wake from this dream that feels so real to me, I stare once again at my swollen feet and realize that we have yet to meet.

For now you live and breathe inside of me, and so you see the love I have for you is very real to me.

So the question is still the same, you see.

Would it, could it, possibly be that I could love you, Joseph, more after we meet?

1 Corinthians 13:13

And now these three remain: faith, hope, and love. But the greatest of these is love.

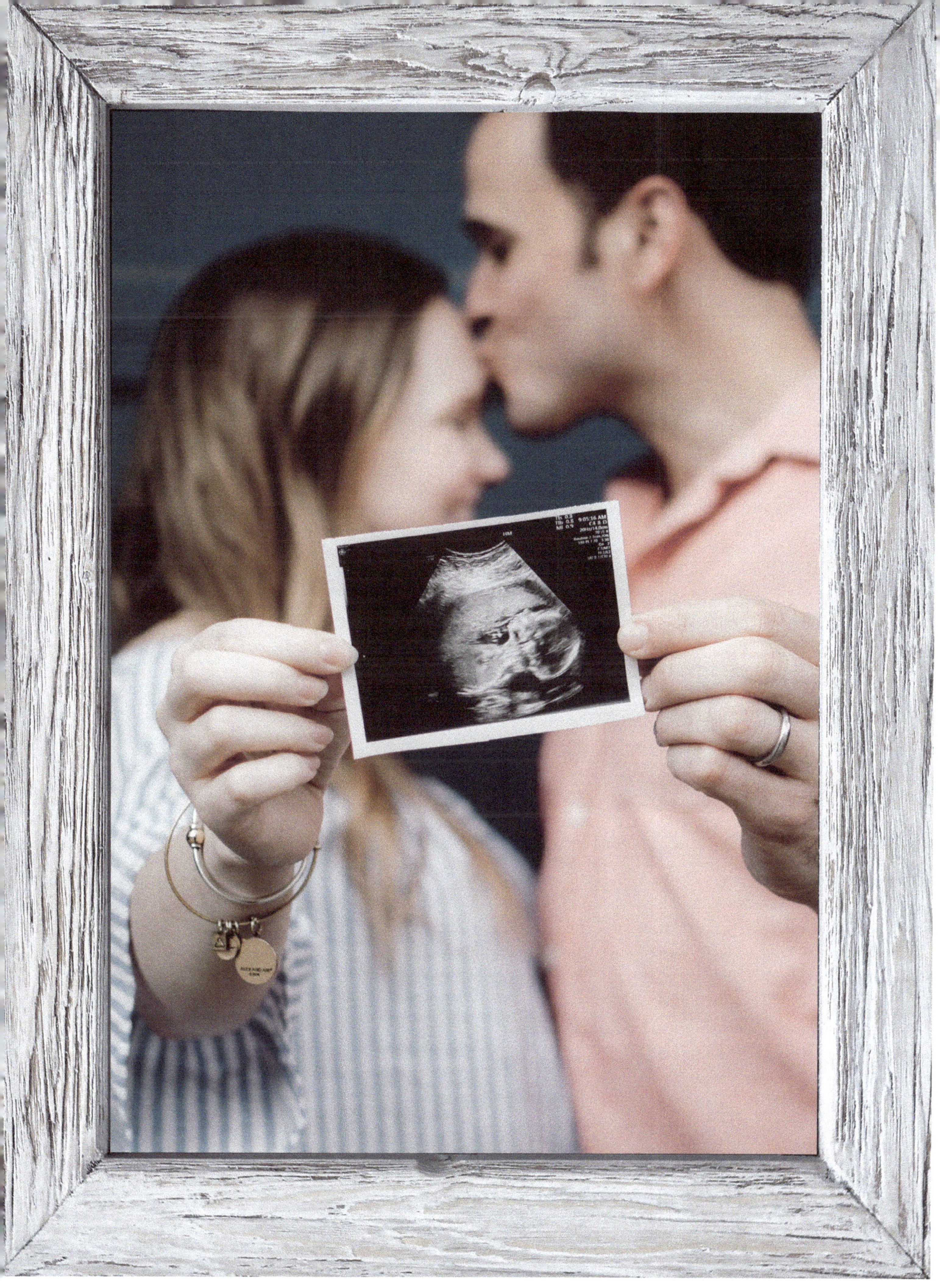

The day you were born

_____
_____
_____
_____
_____
_____
_____
_____
_____
_____
_____
_____
_____
_____
_____
_____
_____
_____
_____
_____

Little Authors

Creating opportunities for children to shine, one Little Author at a time.
Visit us at www.littleauthors.shop or give us a call!

San Antonio, TX (210) 475-3595
Dublin, TX (254) 335-0156

www.ingramcontent.com/pod-product-compliance
Lightning Source LLC
Chambersburg PA
CBHW040141200326
41458CB00025B/6334